HAPPYLAND

POEMS BY KEVIN CONNOLLY

HAPPYLAND

POEMS BY KEVIN CONNOLLY

MISFIT

ECW PRESS

Published by ECW PRESS
2120 Queen Street East, Suite 200, Toronto, Ontario, Canada M4E 1E2

NATIONAL LIBRARY OF CANADA CATALOGUING IN PUBLICATION DATA

Connolly, Kevin

Happyland

ISBN 1-55022-514-6

1. Title.

PS8555.O554H36 2002   C811'.6   C2001-904074-1
PR9199.3.C6377H36 2002

Editor: Michael Holmes, a misFit book
Cover design: Lisa Kiss Design
Text design: Darren Holmes
Production: Mary Bowness
Printing: AGMV
Photography: Marcelle Faucher

This book is set in Bembo

The publication of *Happyland* has been generously supported by the Canada Council, the Ontario Arts Council, and the Government of Canada through the Book Publishing Industry Development Program. Canadä

DISTRIBUTION

CANADA: General Distribution Services, 325 Humber College Blvd., Toronto, ON M9W 7C3

PRINTED AND BOUND IN CANADA

ECW PRESS
ecwpress.com

Contents

UNCLE

3 Uncle
5 More Totality
6 Order Picker
7 Hopeless
9 Pictures of Your Pictures
10 "Symbols Are Lies"
12 Glass Ear
13 Lake, Ocean
15 School Ties
16 Episode
17 Thirteen Verifiable Facts
18 Thanks for the Hat
20 Cummerbund
21 Trench Coat Mafia
22 An Ecology
23 Live a Little

MIDNIGHT ON THE MOON

27 Light and Death
28 East End Incident
30 Grassling
31 Simplex
33 Death is a Daisy
35 The Conversation
38 The Trumped Concerto
39 Safety Verse
40 Amputee
41 Porcelain Jesus
42 Dazzling Slumber

HAPPYLAND

59   IX   Sticks
61   VIII Trial
63   VII Unfortunate
65   VI   P.S. 67
67   V   "Something Bad Got Into Me"
69   IV   Anniversary
71   III "No One Left to Save"
73   II   Miracle
75   I   "Monster"

It's a sad tale,
and no one's guessed a meaning,
a mad call, financed by a loon —
midnight reads the last line.

Last line told in a whisper,
a rumour fueled by hidden sparks,
smothered under weaving maggots —
they ripple over the stiffened bird.

Stiffened bird carried down at midnight,
slender fires winding hidden stairs,
the falcons in their windy stories —
gray years greet them as they wait.

They wait gathered in a rumour,
woven in a wound soothed by soil,
it's a sad tale, conjured by a maggot —
no one lives to hear its end.

UNCLE

UNCLE

I call you my symptom,
my afternoon peach.
I'm your punch-drunk semaphore,
guiding in the under-rotating copters.

Yes . . . I remember it well . . .
glinting like a poor-broke penny
in your bald-floored corral,
last straw used (sucking back a coke),
sawdust squandered (a wet arson's nightmare).

Together we stalk the flaccid hour
with a TV news crew; confused,
clinging to the wind-burned parking lot,
settling on something settled.

We've slipped ham sandwiches
into the condom dispensers,
trussed the emergency exits
with fire hose. Hot-dog vendors
draft terms on napkins
in squeezable yellow mustard.

In the meantime, we're all free agents,
gov docs in designer underclothes,
tapping at the pet-shop glass
with pencils and quarters,
contrary to the explicit
instructions of the proprietors.

At sundown, management surrenders.
There'll be ample time to argue
the rudiments of safe egress,
the relative sentience of the domestic pig —

we'll argue till the cows come home,
dragging their fart-produced ozone holes
like an October tailwind
hauls a Goodyear Blimp —
the "Step Smartly" of Akron, Ohio.

Today I'm seeing grave sites
in the dumpsters, my name
and health card number
gathered quietly, a prize
under the rim of a paper cup.

All crimes are becoming one crime,
these slivers of confluence
just hearsay evidence.
See now, how that one preens,
how this one is erased by doubt.

Sad, blue, sequestered road of cures,
those little empty spaces
no one's thought to walk.

MORE TOTALITY

All he could see
was the end of his nose,
which looked about the same:
a red silk passel of wits
slouching with their backs
against the worms.

Nothing readily expires —
a kiss, a blow,
a milkglass spider —
for everything that scuppers
drop by drop across a windscreen
or a paper door
there's a stubborn odour
in the cigar lounge,
a shabby gathering
on the shivered skin.

Fall draws out all the dormant thoughts:
a green tree bent and flayed
of bark, mossy flagstones,
blood thrilling in a clouding glass.

It praises all the pretty conquests:
warrior flies battered dry
in the chill, sad cats gathered
by a jungle of wires and birds,
the china rim wrestling
with the liquid it gathers.

A drowsy boy conjures
mountains in the nimbus,
then sleeps, while stars groan
and tumble from the light.

ORDER PICKER

CATEGORY FOUR: HORSEMANSHIP

I lose a broken watch,
then dream I am my father.

CATEGORY TWELVE: FIDELITY

The python licks
the cold mirror.

CATEGORY SEVENTEEN: FAITH

A group of flightless birds
admired by thieves.

CATEGORY EIGHTY: AN ANECDOTE

I invent a strange instrument,
motorless and unassembled.

CATEGORY SEVENTY-SIX: ADVANCEMENT

The black hill, a heavy cloud
grasps its own unfolding.

HOPELESS

I'm a sentence.
You're the appeal
to reason —
a worn-out ditty
about the renovation
of a bathroom.

All the little black-clad dogs
are testing mangoes,
cultivating their berets,
assembling complaints —
tiny wizened stalks
for their portfolios.

They've revived
my faith in nothing,
or at least in the nothing
that sticks to the shoes
of the red ants that
scale the concrete slopes
like coffee-pickers,
breaking into small
groups at quitting time,
cheerless and ready for love.

At least it isn't dark just yet.
The seats aren't soggy
with remembered slights.
No one offers up "Thermopolae"
with a weighty tremor.

Still, there's a little cloud
cornered on the plaza
like an idle threat,

battered pockets of rain
drift on the dry line
of the horizon.
Look closely and

you can catch
the darkness moving.
It's advancing,
if I'm not mistaken.

PICTURES OF YOUR PICTURES

Fog sweeps through
the swaying insects,
centres the better dentures.
I arrive and then stop.

A train bends toward
where the storm ended.
Sense, dipped in sleek features,
sinks gratefully into a stone sky.

Why bother the unwed mother?
Sit and spin the glass scraps,
bruise the conductor,
sic the bought bowel
on the flanked blanket,
luggage burning
on an empty platform.

Steam rendered as
a bank of pencil marks,
that photo in dot-screen,
reassembled from memories
of poised noise.

Just count the ways
the body troubles out its odours —
resplendent as the flattened
roadside bingo palace —
pattern, moray, edge.

"SYMBOLS ARE LIES"

he said, or "cymbals are lice,"
but the connection was breaking
up and it was a wrong number
anyway, and I was stringing him along
with noncommittal answers,
pretending when he said,
"Al, my marriage is a mess,"
I'd heard my name instead.
If he found me out later,
I would say he sounded exactly
like a friend in a snowstorm of static,
or a little like a friend I knew
long ago, before puberty even,
and this was how I imagined
his voice would change and how
he would confide in me about
his marriage, if he was in fact
married by now. I mean,
how would I know?

The line was breaking up,
we had what they call
a bad connection, and it occurred
to me that this could be
one of those times you
sort of tuned in
to someone's conversation,
hearing half of it — and then
it bothered me to think
of even my neutral, insincere answers
slipping into nowhere,
while (of course) I missed
the comforting part, the part where
Al was reassuring Len or Dave, or whatever

stranger's name most closely resembles
a friend I could recall quickly, and
maybe rattle off a few details about
when pressed, if only to avoid
the suggestion this was mere voyeurism
on my part, or whatever you call it
when someone intentionally listens in on
someone's private conversation
because they want to know,
they *need* to know, what Al
might have to say about love and betrayal
in these our changing times.

But of course that would be
the part you can't hear,
while what you can hear
is straight and inelegant and familiar,
the kind of dull pain
an aspirin might take care of,
if an aspirin could answer the phone
and be there for a friend,
be there to say, *Take me,*
take me twice. If it's
no better, call Al in the morning.

GLASS EAR

The words that dodge the burning lips
are fraught with timing —
bells and days and rays and bills
pushing this and everything else
into the glass ears we've grown and chipped,
into the pause that feeds the burning,
asking where the fire is,
when the pause stops
being a pause and starts to define us,

climbs our backs, breathing hard,
and chatters in our rented ears,
while the stars shout
and spit dark plates.

LAKE, OCEAN

Put me by the lake and I think ocean,
clams wheezing in the pebbles,
sunned water sizzling like chips.
Sit me near an ocean and I'll squint a lake,
swimmer, smokestack,
salt buried for a million years.

The walk up both cliffs is just
the quickest way to make your heart ache.
From above, everything is itself but smaller —
much smaller, really, hardly worth the trip.

Over in the apartment complex
thugs cart their new belongings
down the fire exits like counterfeit
misery — easily laundered, easily fenced,
the triumph of the cycle over the cyclical.

"Make waves, then pedal your own boat,"
says a little boy they call Gonorrhea.
He's a homegrown nightstick:
no address book, no qualms
and just the one bankable
moment of clarity.

You know what they say —
new daydream, new income —
the rate of interest
as dodgy as the ransom drop.
Clip the digits off with shears
and shape them into letters:
Dear Dad: So far they haven't hurt me.
If only I could say the same for Mom.
The sound of tires — from

the trunk of the getaway car
they hum like incoming jets.

Sketch the control tower,
I'll glimpse the prisoner's sideburns.
Sketch the prisoner and I see the gun.

SCHOOL TIES

"I think it'll work just fine,"
I lie, dirgebuckle coat
loaned like a whore
to a passable thought-mote.

"Serenity is in a pickle,"
the sage sachet stumbles,
bellycertain through the leaves,
stalking raremorning's garnish.

"Hey, bedroom!"
Tot up the stickpins.
"Hey, table-coaster!"
Leave the ring.

Preposterous crumblings,
rot-sprinkled with doubt,
the square bedsheet floating
whole in the airless room.

EPISODE

He craves a different moment,
spies the world-class sorters
boiled with their jackets on,
coffee hissing on their desks.
Pilot errors unboxed and kited —
lazy paper ribbons
drilling in the chilly air.

Chill air piloting a chill sea
buffeting whales singing
their pachyderm show tunes,
tumbling through the cod
amid the glitter of aqueous iceflakes.

There's been an accident at sea,
the too-late churn of rescue ships,
long-delayed hum of turbines
choking on the satellite cut
to Russian women crying on CNN.

A dreamless smudge of sound.
The big, televised launch
of silence into the dark.

THIRTEEN VERIFIABLE FACTS

All the best stuff in Chinese restaurants must be ordered in
Chinese.

You cannot buy property no-money-down.

It is better to be lucky than happy.

It's the astronauts' wives who truly know the moon.

Those little tissue hats never fit.

I love my couch.

The public's right to know outweighs the danger, however
statistically probable, of copy-cat crimes.

I lost my virginity at age 19, two years behind the national
average.

An umbrella dropped is a mitten gained.

Where there's thought, there's mud.

It is possible to hold off the strategic weapons squad of a major
metropolis for 12 hours armed only with a plastic water-gun.

If you open the blinds in a dark room on a bright day, the
half-clad figures inside fade into the air like dust on muslin.

Any self-respecting deity would have stopped the fight long ago.

THANKS FOR THE HAT

The Cathedral of the Arbitrary has never closed
for lack of patrons, there's a good gaggle
most Tuesdays, fresh from the taffy pull,
the Miss Ploughboy contest, the casting call
for *Insert Gambit Here!* — the musical.

I'm sweet on the role of Kip, dogboy
robbed of a magic whistle after falling asleep
for a thousand years. Kip hears the pine ball
vibrate in its little tin prison,
the sound bent by distance and smog,
a fire belch glimmering on the icy skyway.

No matter, the seals arrive anyway,
and Kip's got his sorrow log,
a bucket full of chum and
three-year-lease on
a small stretch of Camp Stench.
"Thanks for the hat!" I rehearse
shouting through my sandwich

as the fair Lenore dives open-mouthed
into the sludge and the dance sequence begins,
minus the midget, minus Telly the
Semaphore King, minus the weasel
with a cap tipped like Rock Hudson,
hair thick with pine and feathers.

Mr. Bitter comes to collect,
wearing a rented parrot suit
and toeing a cardboard letter.
"Sure, we got our cultural treasures,"
the parrot recites (in perfect English),
"our world-class artists,

and worth every damn penny, too.
But answer me this — when was the last time
you saw a decently painted van?"

CUMMERBUND

Don't forget me just because
I felt a valve gasp in your chest,
a breast rest and sidle on my shirt,
and the cloth gust with the skin,
like a flag beating over
the empty schoolyard.

It's October, teeth shiver and the jaunty
shamrock on the motel marquis
quivers out a green mockery.
Your skin could spur a pause in all this,
humid, petaled with silk veins,
little pink lakes brought to the surface
by the killer prom-night punch.

So you'll be late to meet your father,
red-eyed and beer-frowzy,
tossing pop cans through the uprights.
So the morning takes a bluing rush
of nausea and sends it somewhere
where it doesn't seem calamitous any more,
or pitched into the rain
like rice against a window.

No, let's leave the lies to the young
and store things as they were:
impostors scribbled in the motel guest-book,
chill leaves shuttering the streetlight,
shadows ghosting under the bolted door
and the mumbling tree
that coves its arms in darkness,
turns its back,
then dreams us into being.

TRENCH COAT MAFIA

Each millimetre a mile,
though each of those
a memorable if inconsequential stroll
down a rain-littered street.

You rise, then retreat to bed,
wake and renegotiate the pause,
a mouthful of curds, chewing out a barter,
an earful of Serbs, shouting in the lane.

In an age of argument you're the ultimate settler —
no use stumbling over a border —
though the black box babbles,
coughs purple static over the bottles and the blood.

"Happy Earthday!"
the stout tree grumbles
through its paper cells.
Spiders map the palm of doubt,
deaf birds preen and chuckle on the line,

and Heaven's Charm,
the little white-faced darling,
stirs, flushes, gasps,
then winds the warm world
down to dust.

AN ECOLOGY

The aerial view unearths a forest:
the river is a tree;
the streams that feed it, branches.
Shorebirds shimmer on the banks;
their feathers are leaves,
turning on the wind,
their open eyes, pores
shivering with water.
Little boys loom over their
chatterings like storm clouds —

the little stones they pelt
them with are rain.

LIVE A LITTLE

The street is a short leash,
the apartment, a dirty blue ball to chew on.
Down in the city, legions of the sane
stab at the day like it was free cheese.

The cat-skinners stalk the alleys
disguised as art students,
chase mice from mazes,
rehearse grainy, videotaped confessions.

Still, all is not lost:
I have my suspicions,
my stubborn silences,
my dwindling pillbox
of momentary clarity:

the public outcry
I've gathered in a jam jar,
the kid sister who exists only in dreams.
Why not live a little?

Let the dregs of last night's ales
bead on the forehead, then shake
them over your bare toes
like warm rain.

A rose resembles us,
if only in its weakest moments,
and the shadow in the mirror
that moves is me.

MIDNIGHT ON THE MOON

LIGHT AND DEATH

To start, more recent treasons:
the misspent energy of
a smile at the wrong stranger;

a rumble in the garden
behind the clutch of lilacs,
roamy branches scrumming on the tree.

The tiny juniper,
scowling in the poplars,
rustles like a flower girl
in a sea-green dress,
bouncing her heels off a folding chair,
glaring at her little grimy fists.

The yellow light
sets terms for surrender
in the branches, then
rushes the windows,
cuts walkways through the vestibule;

the fogged hills
gasp a fiery trickle
over a glowing rim,
birds doze, then shuffle through the leaves.

A truck engine turns over and
the dreams stiffen and stretch,
running wild and wet as dogs,
rummaging the feast of shadows.

EAST END INCIDENT

Bill might have been blinded like the rest
but he's the proprietor of this
perpetual high-rise yard sale.
He's got broken steam curlers
and chalk outlines to find homes for.
Besides, it's hard work
waking the dead — tucking
the cool limbs into scraps of plaid,
propping them up on lawn chairs
to watch *Oprah* on a blurred TV.

But the cyclist slows to get a glimpse,
while the skateboarder keeps pace
and the tree trunks tick off the cells.
Everything gets all Edward Muybridge
for a while, rare footage played out
like a tongue over Queen East.
The law arrives like an on-cue buzzkill:
the quack of the squad car,
the gathering of fabric around the belt
as they emerge. P.C. Grable stops traffic
while P.C. Huffington runs about frantically,
gathering film from sidewalk,
sewer grates, the fingers
of the stumbling and bewildered.

After typically fruitless interviews
with the local indigents, they
toss the film into the trunk
with the strangled coeds and
half-finished Mike's Hard Lemonades,
and turn the prowler back into the twilight.
Unknown to them, a lone frame
has slipped the dragnet, dodged a hydro pole,

climbed a whorl of brown leaves,
and lodged itself like a knife
between Bill's third and fourth fingers.

Searing, impossibly bright,
it stutters in the heat like a dove.

GRASSLING

On the undercard
Mr. Spectre of Change meets
Mr. Inevitable Comeback of Meat.
Specials rotate every Thursday,
but fish day's always the same.

Consult the bank of brochures in the foyer:
everything popular is gaudy,
the comic sequence of address
distributed free of charge
among the squabbling ruins.

Folk singers have released the minks;
their razored claws churn the countryside
into a rich yet hairy butter,
and a sea of vegans board Corvettes,
(or was it courgettes?) before order is restored.

Ms. Cage of Glory and Miss Missing Link
spit green sequins into the humble pie,
and the options float free again —
repulsed hands drifting in the glorious,
dung-coloured pond, hissing:
This isn't it . . . isn't it . . . isn't it. . . .

SIMPLEX (THE FOLLY)

Burst of colour, just another bead
on the string of missed appointments.
You've lost your reason for the meeting,
still you clutch it darkly, like a match.

Let's take sides: I'm the Constable of Pain,
bylaws bustling like a heavy stream of fish,
you're the Unused Diaper, whet and gasping
against a telephone pole — the same pole

that shoulders the wire that can't stop sagging
under the weight of insensate birds
who won't carry the message
rolled and duct-taped to an acorn

blown from an ancient tree,
sent to the capitol to marry happily,
put on airs, tumble from love,
and die friendless in a
spotless two-room apartment.

Still, the roots abide under the grass
next to the vast gasping lake, friendless itself,
though carved with the frenzied
troths of two centuries of sweethearts.

Best not to linger by the puddle,
its marooned gown of algae, its concerto of sighs.
Against the cool copse, the folly aches,
clapboard vulva ghosted in waning light.

The visitors enter but the friction scatters,
a storm of gulls blown noiselessly
over a grey pate of water.

My mistake, the high-rise whispers,

beloved though uninvited neighbour,
looming as the boathouse groans,
and the swarm of shadows clambers out
its cramped, inevitable choke of dusk.

DEATH IS A DAISY

Death is a daisy
clutched in a sticky child's fingers,
but time is a toad, hunkered in the cooler grass,
not flying but fly-fishing, tonguing the darkness
while the little dears carry on in the sun,
making little fly pyramids, impersonating clouds.

What should any of this mean to me, hunched
over meat loaf in the diner, splitting straws?
I die in my heart exactly twice a day:
this morning, a rag doll tossed across
an Iowa cornfield, and now
in the crippled giraffe I've fashioned

from a folded napkin, teetering precariously
on the lip of a hastily assembled
but nonetheless convincing
chasm of mashed potatoes.
Not that I'm complaining:
apart from these thoughts

my mind is a clear white plain
suitable for sanding, then stucco,
or for assaults on the land speed record
(in which case, skip the stucco).
Screwed to the wall above the lunch counter

the little window chatters out its idiot music.
This is what it knows today:
Spielberg gives the war back to those who earned it;
strippers don't dig garlic;
Elle MacPherson has passed Madonna as most-groped wax
    statue;
corporate America loves it when Johnny Bench sings.

It's midnight on the moon,
stars mutter the familiar cautions,
the leaves misread the cue cards,
strange words wander the freeways like mice.
For now, we'll stick to what's manageable:

those small pornographies usually bought on credit,
the sordid revolutions of tadpole planets,
the singing fingers of the freshly blind,
the butter-breathed cheerleader
crouching in the bushes to pee.

THE CONVERSATION

I am a quiet man,
a gentle giant.
My days adore me,
just ask them —
butter wouldn't melt.

Out there, on the grim
side of the window,
the open-mouthed sacks
sit stacked on the lawn,
waiting to be filled with joy
— not easy joy
cobbled from the mirth of others,
but real joy, hard-earned,
an elation shared by saints.

On the other side of the lawn
there's a hillock. Below that,
a bivouac of elms.
There's a breeze today.
I know this because the trees
dip slightly, leaves turning
over like children's hands —
clean, soiled, clean, soiled —
though the nails are hard to see.

Did I mention the fence?
Perched on the grey slats
this side of the hillock
sits a sorry string of starlings.
They're looking right at me,
gawking, really.
I say, "Baseball."
They say, "Baseball."

I say, "Cupcake."
They say, "Cupcake."
They say, "Barn owl."
I say, "Burn howl."
We're getting exactly nowhere.

Even so, a cloud of bluebottles
drifts over to the picture window,
showing their approval
by bashing their little
fly heads against the glass.
The best applause is always
empty applause.

A group of squirrels
flounces into the picture.
They say "Freedom."
I say, "Firm hand."
They say, "Catechism."
I say, "Crash site."
I say, "Steak knife."
They say, "Spanish sauce."

Just when things are looking
dire, a unicorn clatters
from the shadows of the woods.
I grab a beer and step
outside for a better look.
"Hawk?" I suggest, approaching
with textbook caution.
"Hand-saw," she replies,
going down on one knee.
"Wheelbarrow," I say,
touching her knotted mane.
She says, "Rain water,"
chiding my obviousness.

Then an elm jumps forward,
shedding bark as it goes.
It reveals a mic and a microcassette,
hidden wires tucked
under glued-on leaves.
"There," the elm says smugly,
ridding its trunk of duct tape.
"Argue with that!"

But I am a quiet man,
ask anyone; a resourceful fellow,
admired by many.
The tree's leaves
will be examined for particles of dirt
(and they're plenty dirty),
a cassette will disappear,
improbably, from
the evidence room.

At the inquest, I will deny
everything.

THE TRUMPED CONCERTO
after Lorca

Henri Rat, amorous
bard of the profound keyhole,
left fielder, lying hale and sleepy
in the television's haze.

Processions of sordid Protestants
caress your junkets,
and the rain, smothered on the umbrella,
is inventing cracks in the mud.

Cue the old tavern of fears,
emptied of its sad muscles,
the mice resigned to their detainment,
hope stranded in local history.

We move among bouncers —
their theories of absent landscape,
their big knives and Pythagorian challenges —
like miscast courtiers

cut down by a hundred hands.
Small nourishment thrown at the moon.

SAFETY VERSE

Close one eye and the white sheets rise,
close the other and everything drops
below the window and the rain.

Sister Dawn, relentless, strands
"Twist and Shout" on autoplay.
A plastic shrub is Popeye,
a red wheelbarrow, Olive Oyl,
and Billy Blastoff twists, slippery
in his original packaging.

A late train crests the hill
but never jumps the rules,
Gus Grissom inhales, and
blows his lungs to Kleenex,
while the frogmen bellow
and the air-suits cruise,
cool as dice.

AMPUTEE

The steel door
an anagram for pain —
weak in the knees, a pianist fades.

A singing toy,
a legless woman from Portand,
drunk, on a whim,
buying stockings for her arms.

In front of the church a child is crying.
The door opens, a thought emerges.

PORCELAIN JESUS

and little shampoo Pope,
on a pee break, silhouetted
by your standard frosted window.
His acolyte, Sir Thomas, severed head
toppled over skin cream, bath salts,
an anonymous squeeze bottle.

A trapeze of leggy ivy
brought indoors to duck the cold,
the light show behind it all
storyboarded, crept up from
adjacent basements,
sifting hedge and gravel,
the weeping roof shedding snow.

Bathroom, middle of
the night, light off —
that familiar joust
of the real and the seen
that means everything
and settles nothing at all.

DAZZLING SLUMBER

I

We've weathered the worst,
the sunlight says

dead pots, match-stick houses,
massive slumbering dogs

a hubcap rides the clothesline
of the sideroad

lost coins, gusting bedsheets

II

Winter pays its debt in leaves

stiff jeans, gelid puddles,
hair that hurts

a blue squirrel gambles on
ice-heavy branches

night stirs, bruised wings

III

Nothing scarier than
a half-opened door

steps to the street, water
in the gutter, coughing by the lake

cold bones rake black water
gathering handshakes, heading for home

IV

Midnight rounds up the stragglers

stubborn cinders, gaping boxes,
corridor of aching trees

the storm assembles
its glittering aneurysm

breath's curfew, shrieking ladder of clouds

V

Trucks simmer out the half-light

diesel, desert cedar, wet-dog
scent of tents in the gloom

night storms the plain
on crutches, then

silver knives, sudden cloudburst of stars

VI

The bungalows silent as cue cards

mosquito coil, twitching streetlight,
clash of bottles in the garage

crickets flip the clasps, loosen collars

rusted bicycle, dry legs screaming
in the evening

VII

The ones who need the manual
read the manual

thumb, another digit,
empty shoe, then a full one

for the first time in memory
there are pigeons in the foyer

weather turns, drops
follow each other down

VIII

Moonlight frosts the vacant planet

same face, same scent,
same voice singing in the waves

troughs fill with spectral leaves

same vague light, same mutter
of branches

IX

We'll tough it out, but
it won't be pretty

wet swingset, famished sun,
windy litany of hours

a tongue rolls,
harbours a tepid droplet

bright blooms,
their ancient terrible spikes

X

Regret strolls the jolly mausoleum

plastic armchair, copper thimble,
maundering inventory of dust

the family reconvened as
vintage breathing apparatus

toy wounds, blood beading the stitches

XI

The world is sad and the people are ugly

fate, technocracy, *A Shorter
History of Nineteenth Century Thought*

hope flounces through the nursery
in a blood-caked pinny

the eccentric encore, the singing
grottos of dawn

XII

We're summoned to the crimson funeral

tan line, smudge fire, shivering
bucket of light

a bank of wildflowers lauds
the sordid assignations

curtains and petals,
their minstrel shimmy

HAPPYLAND

All that we do
does not go around in circles.
It is not always the same, no.
Even if we burn up, it's not always the same.
— Hilton Obenzinger, *New York on Fire*

IX
STICKS

In another city they might have
bulldozed it into the ground.
But this is New York,
the building is still sound,
and the loft craze may yet wind
its way through the Bronx
to Southern and East Tremont,
where the Hondurans used to
dance to Los Gaetos Bravos,
Tito Puente and the Garifuna Kids,
drink Cristal and Salavida
and blue sky about home.

At Happyland the single door
remains boarded, the sign
that smiled over the bodies,
shoulder to shoulder, taken down
the day after, the irony
lost on no one, and with everything
else, too much to take.

There's even a memorial,
though rarely flowers — most
of the families went home
after the settlement in '95.
It's ringed by a high fence,
the names etched
onto a concrete obelisk:
Alvarez, Denny; Alvarez, Hector;
Alvarez, Jose; Benavides, Victor. . .

From a distance, they resemble
sticks, or the strokes made by sticks

to stand for numbers:
Castro, Janeta; Chavez, Carla;
Colon, Elias — not frightening in
themselves, just rows of names
with a memory looming over them,
an item list, in inverse order:
obelisk, fence, street,
sidewalk, threshold, boarded
door, hallway, stairwell,
grave.

VIII
TRIAL

The monster arrives in chains.
The tabloids study the face,
maybe fattened a little by prison food,
only the most crazed aspects
good enough for the late editions —
a Christmas shot with Lydia tagged
"Date With the Devil," vilification
of his alleged Cuban offenses,
the old words — *loner, indigent,*
sociopath, drunk — the old arguments:
a parsing of jealousy, the sanity
required to enact the insane.

Nothing to settle but the hierarchy of facts.
Julio, in tears, wakes his neighbour
Carmen Melendez, at 4:15 a.m., says
he's killed Lydia and burned down the club:
I didn't believe him, he was very drunk,
I told him to go sleep it off.
His confession to officers Moroney and Lugo:
We barely asked him questions —
basically he was saying he did it.
His quarrel with Eduardo Porras,
the Amoco station worker who refused
to sell the gas at first, until
a passerby recognized him,
said Julio was okay.
His prints on the plastic oil jug
and a beer can at the scene,
the fracas with the bouncer
and Julio's angry vow to return:
He was drunk and foul-mouthed,
so I threw the maricone out.

His employment troubles and depression,
the six-year relationship with Lydia Feliciano
and the origin of their quarrels,
her objection to his interest in her niece
— a misunderstanding, Julio says —
perhaps an excuse to remove
another burden from her life.

Once sanity is established,
there's little to deliberate —
the victim statements fill phone books.
For the first time in an American courtroom,
a foreman says "guilty" 174 times,
twice for each of the dead.

The verdict takes five minutes to read.

VII
UNFORTUNATE

The sideshow starts a week after
and goes on for months.
Showboat Miami lawyer Ellis Rubin
meets returning mourners
on the tarmac at Tegucigalpa;
The lives of your loved ones
should be worth something, he says,
citing millions in insurance.
The wealthy New York owners
of the deathtrap are identified:
billionaire land speculator
Alex DiLorenzo II, whose father
once owned the Chrysler Building,
Jay Weiss of Little Peach Realty
(a.k.a. "Mr. Kathleen Turner")
juggling class-action suits
from Honduran widows
while his wife wows them
downtown as Maggie in
Cat on a Hot Tin Roof.

Look Brick! How high my body stays on me —
nothing has fallen on me — not a fraction.

Ms. Turner calls the events unfortunate,
but the same thing could
have happened at a MacDonald's.
Rumours of a settlement — some of
the mourners quit jobs
in anticipation of the money —
then the sidestep on a sublease,
the only legally responsible party,
beyond one sorry Cuban,

is Elias Colon, dead with the others.
Condolence cards, signed by
the mayor, arrive two months late.

In the *Law & Order* episode
the club is called El Cielo,
and there's no mention
of wealthy land speculators.
Instead, a corrupt Latino
businessman selling forged green cards.
Five years later the civil suits
settle — after lawyers, about
$7 million divided by 87 families.
Not much muscle in Happyland,
but enough to get home.

VI
P.S. 67

They are trying to be kind
through their bullhorns,
just 20 identified and 67 more —
It's a long process — you'll be
here for hours. If you're not
a relative, please leave.
But Hondurans know about queues,
will join a line to join the line
which creeps one group at a time
into the room with the nutrition
charts and class schedules,
the coffin-rows of Polaroids.

The first family was fine,
an official remembers.
Calm, they even thanked us. . . .
Then the second mother came in
and fell down screaming.
They are offered benches,
tea and vanilla cremes,
mostly they stand: the mothers
and the pregnant, what's left
of the under-25 soccer teams,
visa violators and illegals already
rehearsing the deportation speech.
They should stick them up
on the wall, a woman says.
It would be better than the nerves.

29 widows, two families
completely wiped out —
none of it touches the sleepers
in their little windows,

face matched to face,
finger to photo,

no way out of the frame.

V
"SOMETHING BAD GOT INTO ME"

Call it sleep if you must —
a slender man passed out
on an iron cot, a door opened,
the super with an old cliché:
Nice guy, very quiet, I wouldn't
never expect nothing like this.
Police, questions, a groggy Cuban
half-drowned with fear.

Julio Gonzalez: came with the
Mariel boatlift in 1980, an army deserter
who invented a story about drugs
to make Castro's list of parasites.
Before sponsorship, detention camps:
Fort Chaffee, Arkansas,
Fort McCoy, Wisconsin —
who knew America
could be this cold?

Six weeks after being let go
from the lamp factory, he's
carrying junk to the curb for coins,
washing the windows of cars;
when it's down to food, begging.
I got angry, he tells them,
emptied out. *The devil got in me.*

Sunday afternoon, passed out
in his clothes, in the beige
10 by 12 foot room
he does his best to keep clean.

Four dollars in his pocket,
shoes still rank with fuel,

nothing on the walls but Jesus.

IV
ANNIVERSARY

The jolly face dividing the two
words on the street sign overlooks
the firemen and the sleepers.
Latin slang for America: *Happy Land.*
And underneath: *Little League — Pony,*
For Hire Hall, All Social Events.

The second floor was so stacked with death
the firemen handed bodies through
a hole punched into the wall
of the contractor next door.
Out in the street, some are zipped
into black bags, others doze
under overcoats and firemen's blankets.
For the rest, nothing but a March chill,
a fine layer of soot on wax faces —
the merest kiss of fire, nothing
to nourish even the gawkers.

Mayor Dinkins arrives at 5:30
and leaves the scene ashen; halfway
home he turns the driver around.
Did he really see that?
Or is this another nightmare,
legs tugging at sheets, shoulders waiting
for his wife's dozy caress
from a dead sleep, the touch
that brings him back to earth?
The worst circumstance
I've ever viewed, he tells reporters.
I wanted it etched in my memory.

By the cruelest coincidence,

a firefighter's memorial that same
Wednesday — 79 years to the day since
the Triangle Shirtwaist fire,
the day it rained seamstresses
in Washington Square.

He's heard the story only once
but it comes back on him now:
146 dead, average age 19,
mostly Jewish and Italian,
146 women in a top-floor sweatshop,
doors and stairwells padlocked,
the only way down, the elevator,
so the managers could check for theft.
As the flames spread, they panicked,
tossed themselves down the shaft
after the packed cage, the elevator
operator cranking the stubborn handle,
unable to get back up
through the clog of bodies.

They shimmied out onto
ledges and froze beside blistering
windows, joined hands and
jumped through the smoke.
Those first, then the ones on fire,
landing on wrists, knees,
hitting so hard
it spooks the fire horses.
March 25, 1911:
the day the angels fell

nine floors into heaven.

III
"NO ONE LEFT TO SAVE"

They come into the four-eight around 4:30,
at first just five or six — hysterical, shouting
in Spanish — then a flood through
the station-house door: *Fuego! Muertes!*
a detective shouting about 80 people dead
and within minutes, uniforms with witnesses,
FDNY, the DAs and ADAs, then the press.
I never even made it to the street,
there were just too many interviews
and statements to deal with. We didn't know
what happened. All we knew was
lots of people were dead.

The final blocks up Tremont
they hear nothing from the scene,
just a tepid silence, black trees
flying by like fingers. Once there,
nothing but smoke and fireballs
and hoses — then they spot the DJ
on the pavement, steam coming off him,
speechless, dazed, struggling to get up.
Big heat, but not tough to fight,
the fire spinning in place,
using the building as a flue.

When it's out, more unsettling quiet,
the clatter of boots at the threshold.
Men trained to jump at a moan,
doubled over, shining flashlights,
calling hoarsely into the black socket.
Parts of the staircase intact,
shielded by the human sculpture,
the silence falling through,

cold air streaming under a door.

The first man on the landing kicks
a barstool, then another overturned chair,
tips the flashlight, shouts, too loud —
Better get the fuckin' Captain —
then stumbles on an ankle, keens,
and drops to his elbow among them.

Some looked like they were sleeping;
some looked horrified or in shock.
There were some holding hands,
people who looked like they were
trying to commiserate or hold each other.
Some had torn their clothes off
in their panic to get out.

One litre of gasoline ignited
in the only entrance of the
Happyland Social Club.
No windows, no sprinklers,
no fire route, no emergency lights.
Fire set: 3:30 a.m.
911 called: 3:41 a.m.
First crew arrives: 3:44.
Four survivors, including Lydia
Feliciano, one badly burned.

87 dead, no one left to save.

II
MIRACLE

Like all miracles
it is essentially mindless,
wearing only what
personality we give it:
ravenous, cleansing,
sensate, shrewd.

And like every disaster
it is not one element,
but a painful confluence —
fuel and flame, lung and breath
— a meeting of needs,
an occasion built on threat.

It will sit idle for an hour,
then in a whisper chase
the air up two flights,
cave a corridor in brightness,
skin the room whole, break its ribs
and lick the bones hollow.

The last song Ruben Valladarez
played at Happyland was
Cocoa Tea's "Young Lovers."
Dancers swinging over an inferno —
not enough women, so they move
in arcs, three men to a girl,
or up front facing the DJ.
There would have been little warning,
a faint smell of gasoline; later,
a commotion by the stairwell,
muffled cries of *Fuego! Fuego!*
but by then the only way out was

straight down the monster's throat.

Just one man, the DJ, shouting
encouragement to imaginary followers,
escapes the second floor.
19 made it down one flight,
surfed the tangle on the landing
before being flattened by flames.

The rest died where they stood,
a forest of dancers felled in a stroke,
couples still embracing; a *borachon*
slumped at the bar, fingers
still on his glass, others tumbled,
feet tangled in the barstools,
killed not by smoke or flame but
an idea — poisoned space,
air funneling down — the
sudden absence of something

needed urgently downstairs.

I
"MONSTER"

In your anger you think
you've imagined everything.
Still, you may never get over how easy
it was to let it in, to spread
fire from chest to walls,
a jug pulled from the trash,
a dollar's worth of gas,
a pause by the payphone
to avoid an acquaintance,
then tumble the liquid
like a child spills syrup,
from the stairwell to the lobby
to the coatcheck where you
met your Lydia so many times.

Only the fuel itself is stubborn,
unaccustomed to all that air,
fingernails touching surface
as the physics thuds home.
It never happened, but
you see it vividly,
as you did that morning,
shoes glazed in gasoline,
lingering by the firemen,
close enough to touch them —
Lydia at the coatcheck
dumbstruck, girdled in flames
while the niece dies quietly upstairs.

The devil that came on you is
long gone, barely remembered,
and even then, through others.
A lie told and told again,

like a cancellation — a single fish
buffeting against the many,
a vague chill running over a face
at breakfast, leaving only light.

Wait it out, you think,
next year shorter than the last.
Blur the white walls out
to that empty corridor
we all recall, a passage
booked long ago.
A stage whisper on the
threshold confirms it's that simple:
a door opening on another,
then forget the rest —

this world, all flames.

"School Ties" (page 15) could easily have been titled, "Lines Composed After Reading Too Much Bill Knott."

"Thanks for the Hat" (page 19) is for Gary Barwin and Gregory Boyd Bell (who supplied the last line).

"Cummerbund" (page 20) is pure fantasy. I never went to my high-school prom.

In "Trench Coat Mafia," the line "The stout tree grumbles . . ." is plundered from James Agee.

"Midnight on the moon" (page 33) is after a line by Pierre Reverdy.

"Simplex (The Folly)" (page 31) was written after a long bike ride along the Toronto lakeshore, finishing at the Adamson estate in Port Credit.

"The Conversation" (page 35) owes a debt to Stuart Ross' "Adjustments," James Tate's "Worshipful Company of Fletchers" and poems in Walid Bitar's *2 Guys on Holy Land* (Wesleyan, 1993).

"The Trumped Concerto" (page 38) is a "naive translation" of Lorca's "El Concierto Interrumpido."

In "Dazzling Slumber," the first line of Part XI (page 52) is an inversion of a line by Philip Larkin.

"Happyland" (page 57) was very pointedly inspired by Hilton Obenzinger's *New York on Fire* (The Real Comet Press, 1989), published a year before the East Tremont fire. The poem is modeled on a Roman Catholic *novenario*, a nine-day period of

prayer preceding an anniversary mass. Though "Happyland" is a work of fiction, facts and dialogue are taken from the news reports of the day, and the author would like to acknowledge the outstanding reporting of Bill Keller, Ralph Blumenthal, James Barren, James C. McKinley Jr., Don Terry and Mireya Navarro (*New York Times*); Andy Logan (*The New Yorker*); and Laurie Goodstein
(*The Washington Post*).

Acknowledgements

A few of these poems have appeared in *Who Torched Rancho
Diablo?*, *This Magazine* and in the anthologies *Last Word*
(Insomniac, 1995) and *Blues and True Concussions* (Anansi, 1996).

Special thanks to my editor Michael Holmes for a keen eye,
good ear, and open mind and for literally blackmailing me into
writing this book; Stu Ross (what would I do without you?);
and Gillian Adamson, whose sheer enthusiasm pushed the title
poem into the world. Warm thanks to Lynn Crosbie, who's
sometimes seemed like my fan club of one; Jason Anderson for
the detective work on late '80s Latin dance music; and Lisa Kiss
and Marcelle Faucher for going above and beyond on the cover
and type design.

Thanks also to Michael Redhill, A. F. Moritz, Heidi Greco,
Dennis Lee and Clint Burnham for their attention and
generosity toward past work; Stu and Lynn for lying about this
one; and Jack David, Amy Logan, Darren Holmes, Mary Bowness
and the whole crew at ECW for making this book the fun it
should be.

Finally, thanks to my family and my friends and colleagues at
eye Weekly who, without knowing it, helped awaken Godzilla
from his thousand-year sleep.

The author gratefully acknowledges the generosity of the
citizens of Ontario through the Ontario Arts Council.

ABOUT THE AUTHOR

Born in Biloxi, Mississippi, Kevin Connolly lives in Toronto, where he works as a poet, editor and journalist. He was co-founder of the influential literary magazine *What!* (1985-1993) and edited the Pink Dog chapbook series in the mid-'90s. Connolly's first collection, *Asphalt Cigar*, was a finalist for the 1995 Gerald Lampert Award and he was one of six writers featured in *Blues and True Concussions* (House of Anansi, 1996), an anthology of new Toronto poets.